Living For Jesus

Ross Thompson

Published by Ross Thompson, 2022.

While every precaution has been taken in the preparation of this book, the publisher assumes no responsibility for errors or omissions, or for damages resulting from the use of the information contained herein.

LIVING FOR JESUS

First edition. September 3, 2022.

ISBN: 979-8215542095

Written by Ross Thompson.

Table of Contents

THE FATHER, THE SON, AND THE HOLY SPIRIT WERE PARTICIPANTS IN THE TASK TO SAVE US

GENESIS THIRTY-SEVEN relates the monstrous act of Joseph's brothers. The intention was to murder him. One of the brothers, Reuben, attempted to save Joseph by persuading the others to cast him alive into a pit, with the intention of returning him somehow to his father. Rueben is not among the brothers when a group of Midianite traders pass by. The brothers decide to sell Joseph to the traders. Reuben returns to find he has lost his chance to save Joseph.

Joseph's coat is dipped in goat's blood and taken to Jacob, his father. *"We have found this, is it your son's coat." Then Jacob tore his garments and put sackcloth on his loins and mourned for his son many days. All his children came to comfort him, but he refused to be comforted. "No," he said, "I will continue to mourn until I join my son in the grave." So, his father wept for him.*

Have you noticed something unusual about this passage? Jacob had a relationship with God. As far as we can tell God did not tell Jacob Joseph was not dead. The experience caused great suffering for Jacob. What was happening here? This is what I think. God the Father honoured Jacob by allowing him to share in the sufferings the Father experienced when Jesus died.

Paul expected suffering as a part of his Christian life. *I want to know Christ and the power of His resurrection and the fellowship of His sufferings, being conformed to Him in His death.* (Philippians 3:10) He also said in Romans eight; *And since we are his children, we are his heirs. In fact, together with Christ we are heirs of God's glory. But if we are to share his glory, we must also share his suffering.*

The early Church had a different attitude from what prevails today. *They called the apostles in and had them flogged. Then they ordered them not to speak in the name of Jesus and let them go. The apostles left the Sanhedrin, rejoicing because they had been counted worthy of suffering disgrace for the Name.* (Acts 5:40,41)

Both of those verses and others in the New Testament refer to God's or Christ's suffering. Here is my point. To whatever degree, both God the Father and the Holy Spirit suffered because of what Jesus had to go through to save us. Obviously, it does not need proving that God, who is love itself, would suffer in giving up His Son Jesus to the suffering of Calvary. The New Testament also says, *But Christ offered himself to God without any flaw. He did this through the power of the eternal Holy Spirit.* (Hebrews 9:14) Do not think it did not cost the Holy Spirit a great deal to do that task.

The Gospel of Jesus deserves our respect as we reflect on these facts. How do we understand a God willing to go so far to save us? How does a being who is called love, set themselves to follow through on those activities? Let us never fail to give thanks.

LIVING IN THE ETERNAL FOURTH DIMENSION

The Christian life is spiritual. I believe having a clear understanding of what constitutes who we are as Christians in this life on Earth is the first step towards living well as Christians. To my mind, the metaphor of the third and fourth dimensions clarifies things. Living in the fourth dimension is the life in Christ. We cannot see the fourth dimension with our physical eyes. 2Corinthians 4:18 gives us the basics of Christian living as it is revealed in the New Testament. *...while we do not look at the things which are seen, but at the things which are not seen. For the things which are seen are temporary, but the things which are not seen are eternal.*

Have you noticed how that verse contradicts itself? Paul advises that instead of looking at what is seen, we should focus on what cannot be seen. How does one view something that cannot be seen? This is the starting point for the spiritual life in Christ. Our source of spiritual life is the Bible. The door is faith (trust in what God has said). We access the spiritual life found in the Bible through faith. Faith is imperative. It is possible to have a complete knowledge of the Bible, and no spiritual life, because faith was not practiced.

Living in the Spirit is always about things that last forever. Everything physical/material is transient (passing, short-lived). Romans 8:10 adds more detail. *Your body is dead because of sin, but your spirit is alive because of righteousness, if Christ is in you.* Consequently, good judgement, or common sense, advises putting less emphasis on what is dead, and more emphasis on what is alive

I have to admit that reading comments on Medium (I have a page of articles on Medium) with subject lines "why I am no longer a Christian," "I have a friend who no longer identifies as a Christian," and "I was a Pastor, now I am not a Christian" disturbs me. Whatever their Christian experience, these folks never got to the place of discerning where life and death are. They have chosen death and seem to think they have made some sort of progress. Why would you walk away from life?

The good news is, when we are born again, we automatically obtain spiritual life. (Romans 8:9) *However, you are not in the flesh but in the Spirit, if indeed the Spirit of God dwells in you. But if anyone does not have the Spirit of Christ, he does not belong to Him.* Moving forwards from that point is crucial. John's Gospel 1:12 says, *but as many as received him (Jesus), to them he gave power to become the sons of God, even to them that believe on his name.* The becoming is up to us.

Paul teaches us how to progress from that beginning. *For those who live according to the flesh think about the things of the flesh, but those who live according to the Spirit, about the things of the Spirit. For the mindset of the flesh is death, but the mindset of the Spirit is life and peace.* (Romans 8:5–7)

Our bodies are the temporary carriers on this Earth, of our spiritual life. Our job description is to increase in the life that cannot be seen.

CHRISTIAN LIVING: THINKING MAKES IT SO

The new spiritual life we receive when we are born again includes a new booster for our minds. The New Testament calls it 'the mind of Christ.' Paul, in Romans 8, called it 'the mind of the Spirit'. Another section of the New Testament exhorts us to 'let this mind be in you that was in Christ Jesus.'

The thing with the booster is, that we must use it. If we do not use it, we will find ourselves thinking like the unsaved population. Totally preoccupied with self, we will think of money as they do, we will think about our health as they do, we will think about all the experiences of life that come our way as non-Christians do. The New Testament calls that the carnal mind. The carnal mind does not trust God, believe in God, or submit itself to God.

Kenneth and Gloria Copeland, in one of their books, put it this way; The carnal mind is the mind not regulated by the Word of God. The Word of God regulate the mind of the Spirit. The New Testament describes those without Christ as, in the World without God, and without hope. They live by just crossing their fingers for the best to happen. They have no foundation for expectancy good or bad.

We on the other hand use our booster to live by the helmet of the hope of salvation. Salvation covers all God helps us with in this life. I had to learn this lesson again very recently. I found myself lying in hospital, somewhat bewildered, and irritated at the number of times needles were being poked into my arm to extract blood. After a few hours, the Holy Spirit spoke two words to me; 'believe and receive.' I knew what the Lord meant. Believe the Word of God and receive it into your life. Both are done by speaking.

Those words were all I needed to get back on track. I said, "Lord your Word tells me I was healed by the stripes of Jesus - past tense. It also says you are the Lord who heals me. I believe those words to be true, and I receive them into my life now. "

The tests revealed nothing amiss. All that was stopping the Doctors sending me home was a discrepancy in my blood pressure lying down and standing. My blood pressure would drop when I stood. Standing and laying tests were done five times overnight. Four showed a drop and one a rise in blood pressure when I stood. The question was asked every time, "do you feel dizzy when you stand?" To which I replied "no.'

By that time, I was not interested in results either way. God had told me how to manage the situation and I had done it. That sort of confession of faith only needs to be done once or twice a day. When morning came, they sent me home, after putting 1000 mgs of hydrating drip in me during the night. God had reminded me to use my mind booster and apply the Word of God. We should always avail ourselves of the benefits of medical practice, and never forget to incorporate the truth of the Word of God with it.

God seems to have presented Kenneth and Gloria Copeland as examples of how to live by faith. If you wish to learn about the topic, they have books available online, most of which are only a few dollars. The books are encouraging and present a balanced view of the life of faith.

THE GOOD THINGS HAVE COME

I wonder how many Christians could give an accurate response if asked about the good things to come mentioned in Hebrews 10:1. *The old system under the law of Moses was only a shadow, a dim preview of the good things to come, not the good things themselves. The sacrifices under that system were repeated again and again, year after year, but they were never able to provide perfect cleansing for those who came to worship.*

The context of the verse and those following, is Jesus' provision of the good things to come; perfect cleansing. Also stated as the taking away of sins. Some would say what is meant here is a positional state. The taking away of sins from the believer, positionally in the eyes of God. Others see it as speaking of the doorway to heaven being opened through the blood of Jesus. It includes both those things, but that is not the main meaning of these verses.

What is being discussed here is the removal of sins in this life on Earth. In the here and now. In your daily life and mine. The sacrifices offered by the Priests under the law each day were not enough to take away sin from the people. The context is the people's daily life on Earth. Paul says if the activity of the law could take away sin, the people would have been perfectly cleansed in their daily experience. But, says Paul, it is not possible for the blood of bulls and goats to accomplish that cleansing.

Something else was required. That something was the sacrifice of Christ. Jesus' sacrifice made the taking away of sins possible in this life. Perfect cleansing became available in this life for all who will believe. The context of these verses is the once for all taking away of sins in this life; in the here and now. This wonderful gift from Jesus is what is meant by the good things to come. God is practical. People need deliverance from sin now. Jesus gave us what we need.

For whatever reason, some have tried to bypass the proper context of these verses. They have attempted to move the meaning to the future, or to a sort of pie-in-the-sky positional thing. The context of these verses is the permanent removal of sin from your life and mine, right here and right now. The enemy has worked hard to confuse believers on these points. Our victory lies in embracing the simple Word of God, clearly laid out in the pages of Hebrews, and other parts of the New Testament.

WHAT DOES 'TAKE AWAY SINS' MEAN?

*T*he next day John saw Jesus coming toward him and said, "Look, the Lamb of God, who takes away the sin of the World "(John 1:29) The original language for 'takes away' here, means to lift up, raise, remove.

Day after day every priest stands and performs his religious duties; again and again, he offers the same sacrifices, which can never take away sins. But this man, (Jesus) after he had offered one sacrifice for sins forever, sat down on the right hand of God. (Hebrews 10:11,12) The original language for 'takes away sins' here means to remove, unveil, cast off.

To accurately explain the New Testament statement 'take away sins,' it is necessary to look at the New Testaments' description of the process by which it happened. It is simply explained. The difficult part was all Jesus had to go through to give it to us.

2 Corinthian 5:21 has the essential truth. *Him (Jesus) who knew no sin He (God) made to be sin on our behalf; that we might become the righteousness of God in Him.* Though He had never committed a sin, Jesus was made to be sin so that He could carry it into the penalty of death. Having accomplished payment of the legal penalty of sin on our behalf, He was then raised from the dead because death could not hold him personally. He had never sinned.

We can now see the meaning of 'take away sins' revealed in the New Testament. A genuine believer in Christ's salvation receives that 'taking away of sin.' Sin no longer exists in that person. How could it when Christ has taken it away? Which is why 2 Corinthians 5:21 goes on to say, *"that we might become the righteousness of God in Him (Jesus).* We are now a completely new person. We are described as 'becoming the righteousness of God in Him.'

Becoming speaks of the whole person. A complete transformation. The verse below from Zechariah describes Jesus taking away sin in a single day, applicable to every genuine believer's life, here and now on Earth.

Notice the stone I have set before Joshua; on that one stone are seven eyes. I will engrave an inscription on it, "this is the declaration of the Lord of Armies, and I will take away the iniquity of this land in a single day." (Zechariah 3:9)

HIGH PROFILE CHRISTIAN TEACHER CONFIRMS FALLACY OF THE TWO NATURES ERROR

I was happy to read in a small book by Kenneth Copeland this week, about his rejection of the two natures in the believer error. Here is some of what he says on the topic. I am employing the principle taught by Paul in 2Timothy 2:2 *You have heard me teach things that have been confirmed by many reliable witnesses. Now teach these truths to other trustworthy people who will be able to pass them on to others.* I pass these truths to dependable people who will be able to teach others also.

The small book, available from Kenneth Copeland.org and online retailers is, *Now Are We in Christ Jesus.*

Quote: Being in Christ Jesus makes you a new creature, or a new creation. The literal Greek text says a new species of being which never existed before. When you become a new creature, your spirit is completely re-created. Old things are passed away, all things become new. and all things are of God. You need to realize that you are not a spiritual schizophrenic — half God and half satan. You are all God.

The problem area is not in your spirit, it lies in your mind and body. It is every believer's responsibility to take God's Word and renew the mind. Then he/she can use that Word to control the body. In Paul's letter to the Ephesian Church, he was explaining to them that they had been delivered from their sinful flesh and had been recreated in righteousness. However, it was their responsibility as an act of their will to put on the new man in Christ and stop the works of the flesh.

Just knowing you have been made the righteousness of God in Christ is not enough. You need to have a full understanding of what righteousness is, and what it means to you as an individual believer. Sincere Christians are living far below their privileges in Christ simply because they do not understand their place as a child of God. Righteousness is one of the most vital areas in the Christian walk. Without a knowledge of righteousness, you will never obtain all that is yours in God. **End of Quote.**

I want to leave you with a challenge. If we have been Christians for a while, it is easy to fall into complacency and passivity regarding God's Word. Sitting listening passively to somebody else talking every Sunday can also have that effect. The challenge: take the verse that tells us we are the righteousness of God in Christ. Meditate on it this week. Think of the enormity of that statement. Perhaps ask God to open the eyes of your understanding on the subject. Most of all begin saying it of yourself and believing it of yourself.

Be warned though, it may catapult you into a life you never dreamed of.

SAY NO TO NEGATIVE CHRISTIANITY

What do I mean by negative Christianity? Proponents of negative Christianity will always talk about sin. They will never, and I mean never, face and acknowledge the positive verses about our Christian lives in the New Testament. I am writing about this, not out of any sense of vendetta, but because an understanding of positive Christianity is imperative for a successful and enjoyable experience with God and must be passed on to new believers. The negative Christianity people will never talk about holiness, purity of believers, freedom from sin, (Et al) because they do not understand the topics.

They bypass those verses or make an excuse for them, because they throw a spanner into their theological beliefs. I recently put a selection of the New Testament statements about the purity of believers in a story. I received a comment "Oh that does not mean we are pure; it means God's desire for us is purity." The truth about that is all God's desires for us are given to us through Jesus' atonement. If you get too positive from the New Testament, the negative Christianity person will always warn you about falling into pride, and again, fail to acknowledge the positive passage. For them, Jesus' atonement only gets us to heaven. It does nothing for us in this earthly life.

To some degree they are sincere, but when you ignore the totality of what is said about the condition of Christians in the New Testament, well……. It seems sometimes they have made a commitment to their ideas regardless of what the Word of God says. Perhaps they do not want to face the fact they have been wrong on these issues all their Christian lives.

We are not called to fall in love with a particular theory. Our call is to conform our thoughts to the clear Word of God. At the very least we should acknowledge the New Testaments declarations about holiness, purity, and freedom from sin, even if we do not understand them. Those verses should spark us to begin an investigation and a conversation with God.

There is some negativity in the New Testament. But it comes with a positive attachment. It can be summed up with this phrase; "do not live after the flesh but after the Spirit." We do not have to live as we did before we were saved. We have a new spiritual life. Our bodies are yet to be changed. We learn to live a spiritual life, and keep the body in its place,

I think almost everybody begins the Christian life in negative Christianity. When you have been a resolute sinner, and discover how wrong you have been, it's natural to have some fear of God. It takes a while to be established in the fact that God has always loved you and has paid for your sins through the blood of Jesus. That was my experience anyway. It was some time before I noticed statements about the marvellous things Jesus has given us. Me pure?? Me holy?? I could not discount that information though and had to investigate it.

God is ultra-positive. 2Corinthians 1:20 says; *For all the promises of God in Him (Jesus) are Yes, and in Him Amen, to the glory of God through us.* Here is positive information from the New Testament that will change your ideas about yourself.

...And from Jesus Christ, who is the faithful witness, and the first begotten of the dead, and the prince of the kings of the earth. Unto him that loved us and washed us from our sins in his own blood, and hath made us kings and priests unto God and his Father; to him be glory and dominion for ever and ever. Amen. (Revelation 1:5,6,)

More information about this status we have in Jesus is in Revelation 5:9,10. It underscores the necessity to know all the Word of God. I had not paid attention to this passage until I recently heard a preacher mention it. *And they sung a new song, saying, 'You are worthy to take the book, and to open the seals thereof: for you were slain, and have redeemed us to God by your blood out of every kindred, and tongue, and people, and nation; And have made us kings and priests to our God; And we shall reign on the earth.'* The saints, not in heaven, but reigning on the earth! When will we reign on the earth? For how long? Will it be permanent? What about heaven? I will leave you with that raw material for an investigation of a Bible mystery.

TONGUES, THE SECRET WEAPON

Jesus said one of the signs following believers would be speaking in new tongues. "New' in the original Greek means fresh, new, unused. (Mark 16:17) The New Testament teaches three variations of speaking in tongues. The group from the upper room, on the day of Pentecost, spoke in known languages they had not learned after the Holy Spirit came. The listeners, men from 'every nation under heaven,' heard God glorified in their own language. They marvelled at this sign from the Holy Spirit, knowing the speakers were Galileans who were not multi-lingual.

Throughout the history of the Church, many unbelievers have received the same sign; an unlearned foreign language spoken by a Christian, understood only by the listener.

1Corinthians 14:2 explains what is taking place in the other two variations of speaking in tongues. *For he who speaks in an unknown tongue does not speak to men, but to God. Indeed, no one understands him; he utters mysteries in the Spirit.* When this happens in a Church gathering, the Holy Spirit will give the interpretation of the tongue to another person in the congregation, enabling all to understand what has been said. Personal prayer in tongues without interpretation is strongly promoted in the New Testament. Oral Roberts believed we can ask God for the interpretation of our personal prayer in tongues.

Sometimes, but not always, I have a sense of what I am praying about in tongues. Personal praying in tongues was Apostle Paul's secret weapon. *I thank God that I speak in tongues more than all of you.* (1Corinthians 14:18) *A person who speaks in tongues is strengthened personally, but one who speaks a word of prophecy strengthens the entire church.* (1Corinthians

14:4) Jude says praying in the Spirit (tongues) will strengthen our faith and keep us practicing the love of God. (Jude 1:21)

There is something about praying in the mystery of tongues, which gets the job done quicker and easier than praying in our own natural language. Do you need a breakthrough in an area of your life? Try praying about the situation in tongues. You will sense in your spirit that now, at last, you are getting somewhere.

I have to work at remembering to pray in tongues. Sometimes the Holy Spirit will bring it to my mind, but more often than not it is left to me to remember to use the weapon. I once spent a harrowing month in hospital undergoing serious surgery. It was not until I returned home to finish recuperating, that I realized I had forgotten to pray in tongues the entire time I had been in hospital. Praying in tongues at home helped me to recuperate quickly. I believe my sojourn in hospital would have been easier had I remembered to use my spiritual prayer language.

GOD WAS WITH SAMUEL, AND LET NONE OF HIS WORDS FALL TO THE GROUND

Samuel was dedicated to the Lord from childhood. Much could have been said about his relationship with God, but the Old Testament chooses to focus on one feature. God let none of his words fall to the ground. As far as I can tell that means God kept Samuel from any faults in his speech. The message seems to be; what we say is vitally important.

James said our words (tongue) are like the rudder of a boat influencing our whole being. A Psychologist has suggested it is to our benefit to refrain from using words like 'try' 'I ought to' 'I should' 'I might' 'I may' in certain contexts because they give our bodies an indecisive message. This week somebody said to me "I wish I could paint." that gave a message of frustration to the body. That person would have been better saying; "I could learn to paint if I wanted to." "I should go on a diet" gives an indecisive message to the body. It is better to say, "I will decide to go on a diet soon." We give messages to our minds and bodies when we speak. It is better to be positive and concise in our speech.

A neurosurgeon states the speech centre of the brain dominates all our nervous systems. Our nerves and feelings will respond to our speech whether negative or positive. If we constantly say, "I am worried about (so and so) situation" or "I am so unhappy," the body will attempt to line up with the 'truth' we have spoken. I have discovered I can change my experience merely by speaking. For example, if I make a habit of regularly saying "I am not easily offended" that will tend to become my experience. "I love those people in Christ" becomes a dominant response in my personality if I make a habit of saying it.

I have obtained rest and peace in myself just by speaking out the response to life I want. Regularly saying "I am a friendly person" has worked wonders for me. It works best when what is said cuts diagonally across what you are feeling. Everything is going wrong? "I am a patient person." Feeling anxious, nervy, frustrated? "I am emotionally calm and balanced" "I respond to life and living in a steady sound-minded way." "I am a happy person." It may feel like a waste of time at the beginning, but eventually, you will notice your mind and body have taken the message on board

Pastor David Yonggi Cho suggests we have a positive confession whenever possible. "I am healthy," "I am a blessed person," and "I am victorious in Christ." He says we will change ourselves if we speak productivity, success, exuberance, enthusiasm, and winning in Christ, whenever we can - regardless of external circumstances. I was the sort of person who did not say much. I hoarded everything up in my mind. I do not do that these days. I have found it so much easier to live, if I declare to my mind and body, words that produce health and energy.

SIN NATURE IN BELIEVERS TEACHING, SUBVERTS THE TRUTH

I have no doubt those who hold the sin nature in believers teaching are sincere, although I do think they close their eyes to the many statements about the purity of believers in the New Testament. I have read one or two books where a prominent Christian leader quotes Jeremiah 17:9 *(The heart is deceitful above all things, and desperately wicked; who can know it?)* as the inner condition of Christians. That is just not true.

I do not know where the sin nature in believers teaching originated. Its intention was to devalue or undermine the atonement of Jesus. The atonement itself cannot be touched, but the teaching's intent was to sow deceit and doubt in the minds of believers, regarding the full benefit of Jesus' suffering, death, burial, and resurrection, on our behalf.

Jesus confirmed Jeremiah 17:9 in Mathew 15:19; *"For out of the heart come forth evil thoughts, murders, adulteries, sexual immorality, thefts, false testimonies, slanders."* It is important to recognize here that Jesus is speaking before His atonement became available. He is describing the condition of the heart of all Human beings who do not have His salvation. Luke 22:20 *("In the same way, after the supper he took the cup, saying, "This cup is the new covenant in my blood, which is poured out for you.")* The new Covenant, Jesus' atonement, started at His death on the cross.

If we turn to Acts 15:9 we read of the condition of the heart of those who have embraced Christ's atonement; (Peter speaking) *"He (God) did not discriminate between us and them, for he purified their hearts by faith."* Peter says the first Gentiles to be saved and the Disciples in the upper room on the day of Pentecost received a pure heart from Christ's atonement.

The first Christians knew nothing of an indwelling sin nature. Christ had made them pure inside. Their testimony rings out through the entire New Testament.

Titus 2:14 *"(Jesus) who gave Himself for us, that He might redeem us from all lawlessness and might purify to Himself a people specially chosen, zealous of good works."*

Titus 1:15 *"To the pure [in heart and conscience] all things are pure, but to the defiled and corrupt and unbelieving nothing is pure; their very minds and consciences are defiled."* Notice here there are only two groups of people: the pure in heart and unbelievers.

1Peter 1:22 *"Since you have purified your souls by obedience to the truth so that you have a genuine love for your brothers, love one another deeply, from a pure heart."*

Hebrews 10:1,2 *"The law is only a shadow of the good things to come - not the realities themselves. For this reason, it can never, by the same sacrifices repeated endlessly year after year, make perfect those who draw near to worship. For then would they not have ceased to be offered? For the worshipers, once purified, would have had no more consciousness of sins."*

Ephesians 1:4 *For he (God) chose us in him (Christ), before the foundation of the world, to be holy and blameless in love before him."*

I conclude this section with **quotes** from the sermons of John G Lake. Apostle to Africa and founder of the Spokane Washington Healing Rooms.

"The salvation of Jesus was a redemption of the whole man from all the power of sin, every whit - sin in the spirit, sin in the soul, sin in the body."

"God's first purpose is to make man good by removing the consciousness of sins from his soul, in order that he may grow up into

God and fulfil the great purpose that God has in store for him, becoming a Son of God in mind, nature, power, and capacity to bless."

"Holiness is the character of God. The very substance of His being and essence of His nature is purity. The purpose of God in the salvation of mankind is to produce in man a kindred holiness, a radiant purity, like unto that of God Himself. If God were unable to produce in him such a purity, then His purpose in man would be a failure, and the object of the sacrifice of Jesus Christ would be a miscarriage instead of a triumph."

"There is a consciousness that seems to me by the Word of God and by my own personal experience to be possessed where any individual can enter into the direct presence of God and receive the baptism of the Spirit. That is the consciousness of sinlessness — the consciousness that your sins are gone"

"Jesus purposed to make your heart and mine just as sweet and lovely and pure and holy as His own. That is the reason He can accept the Christian as His bride. Who could imagine the Christ accepting Christians polluted, defiled, of a lower state of purity or holiness than His own?" **End of Quotes**

DIVINE APPOINTMENTS ARE COMING

Two weeks ago, I had a Thursday, 11.30 a.m. doctor's appointment. I slept through the alarm and woke late. I cancelled the appointment and headed to my neighbourhood mall to get groceries. After completing my shopping, I made the decision to unwind with a hot chocolate before going back home.

I had bought my hot chocolate from the coffee shop, and I was sitting close to the front door. An old gentleman arrived in one of those motorized wheelchairs. The back of the chair had a mount for a walking frame, but he chose to forgo it for the short distance into the coffee shop. A few minutes later I noticed he was making for my table, precariously balancing a large cup of coffee in one hand, and grabbing whatever was nearby for support. I offered to take the coffee and placed it opposite me on the table. He sat down and we started talking.

He had lived an exciting life and was 92 years old. He had spent the majority of his working life in the Australian Army, where he had also met his wife. Later in the Army Reserve, he had served as a Major. His time in the army enabled him to travel to many countries, including Vietnam for a brief time during the war.

Somewhere in the conversation, I mentioned I was a Christian. He said he was reading an astronomy book with God in the title. During our conversation, I was able to talk to him about the Gospel and recommended receiving Jesus, particularly for a man of his age. He told me, that every night, he read his astronomy book and a daily devotional book by Robert Schuller. It was obvious he was not a Christian though.

I was surprised later to find we had talked for almost two hours. I left him knowing I had something to pray about. Robert Schuller never fails to explain how to receive Jesus in his books. I asked God that as my friend read it would come to his awareness to put faith into action and ask Christ into his life.

It was not until much later that I realized I had been manoeuvred into a Divine appointment. Not getting to the Doctor, deciding to relax with a hot chocolate, and the fact the old gentleman had decided for the first time in months to travel the three kilometres to the shopping mall, had all been part of the making of a Divine appointment.

My part was to be alert and ready to talk about the Gospel when the opportunity presented itself. The book with God in the title was a good opening, as was our sharing our life experiences. Divine appointments are coming to each of us. A mindset of readiness will enable us to have the joy of passing on the best message of all.

WHO WERE ANGELS OF THE SEVEN CHURCHES IN REVELATION?

The mystery of the seven stars that you saw in my right hand and of the seven golden lampstands is this: The seven stars are the angels of the seven churches, and the seven lampstands are the seven churches. (Rev 1:20)

The original Greek for 'Angels' in this verse means 'Angel, a Messenger.' All the Commentators agree it refers to the Pastor, Bishop, or Overseer of each of the seven Churches. A mystery remains then, as to why the word Angel is used.

Barnes Commentary says: It is evidently implied that the meaning of these symbols would be beyond the ordinary powers of the human mind to arrive at with certainty, and hence John was directed to explain the symbol. The general and obvious truths which they would serve to convey would be that the ministers of the churches, and the churches themselves, were designed to be lights in the world, and should burn clearly and steadily.

The common meaning of the word may be employed to denote anyone who is a messenger, and hence, with propriety, anyone who is employed to communicate the will of another; to transact his business, or, more remotely, to act in his place — to be a representative. **Unquote**

Barnes thinks it cannot mean literally an angel, as referring to a heavenly being, for no such being presided over these churches. He also makes a good point in saying the term may have been deliberately used to convey the respect and authority of the office in God's eyes. The Lord was underscoring the fact the Leader was a heavenly appointment. The spiritual state of some in the Churches may have included disdain for the overseers. This was not a message from the man, but from heaven and the Lord through him.

The Bible references the Lord upholding His people and strengthening them with His right hand. The stars and the lampstands are in the Lord's right hand, receiving support and strength. The stars, as Angels from Heaven, do not fit with this theme in Scripture.

Fear thou not; for I am with thee: be not dismayed; for I am thy God: I will strengthen thee; yes, I will help thee; yea, I will uphold thee with the right hand of my righteousness. (Isaiah 41:10)

THE LAST TWELVE VERSES OF MARK'S GOSPEL PROVED GENUINE

Probably most Christians have heard, at one time or another, the query regarding the genuineness of the last twelve verses of Mark's Gospel. It seems to have come out of the so-called Higher Criticism Movement of the late 1800's early 1900's when a few made a name for themselves by challenging the genuineness of various parts of the Bible.

Ivan Panin (1855–1942) was exiled from Russia at 18 years old. He reached the United States at 22 years of age, where he entered Harvard University to study languages (Greek and Hebrew) and literature. He graduated with a Master of Literary Criticism. Panin was an agnostic who held ideas similar to those of the authors of Higher Criticism.

In 1890 while reading the New Testament Book of John, he noticed what seemed to be a system of mathematical relationships running through the text. His subsequent study of the discovery resulted in his conversion to Christianity in 1891. (Presumably, he had been reading the Greek text which has a number value for every letter - as does the Hebrew of the Old Testament) By this time he was a familiar public figure, and his conversion was proclaimed widely in the Newspapers.

Panin responded to a challenge in the Newspapers for a Christian to prove the last twelve verses of Mark were authentic. He did it mainly by showing the twelve verses are consistent in their mathematical relationships, with the rest of the New Testament. Following is some of Panin's proof sent to the Newspaper.

(As an example of the numbering system; the Greek letters of the word for Jesus have the number values of 10,8,200,70, 400,200 — adding up to 888)

The Bible number 7 stands for perfection and abundance.

The number of words in the verses is 175 or 25x7 divided into 56 words or 8 x7 spoken by Jesus and leaving 119 words or 17x7. These 175 words have three natural divisions - verses 9–11 having 35 words or 5x7/ verses 12–18 having 105 words or 15x7 / verses 19–20 having 35 words or 5x7

The spoken words are 98 or 14x7. These words have 553 letters or 79x7. 294 or 49x7 are vowels - 259 or 37x7 are consonants. 84 of the words or 12x7 are found elsewhere in the book of Mark. 14 words or 2x7 are found only in these verses. 42 or 6x7 of the words are used by Jesus in His discourse to the disciples. 56 words or 8x7 are left

The numeric value of the whole passage is 103,663 or 14,809 x 7. The numeric value of the first division by letters is 17,213 or 2,459 x7. The rest of the passage's numeric value is 86,450 or 12,350 x7

Non-nouns in the passage are 77 or 11x7. Nouns 21 or 3x7 of which seven begin with a vowel and 14 or 2x7 begin with a consonant. The word that occurs most in the vocabulary of the passage occurs 21 times or 3x7. Its number value is 70 or 10x7. One word in the vocabulary of this passage 'deadly' (in the Greek) appears nowhere else in the New Testament. Its numeric value is 581 or 83x7. This word is preceded in the vocabulary by 42 words or 6x7. And preceded in the whole passage by 126 words or 18x7.

The first and last words in the passage have numeric values divisible by seven. In the passage, Jesus appears to Mary, two disciples, and the eleven =14 or 2x7.

Panin authored a book on his proof of the last 12 verses of Mark (and other books dealing with Bible Numerics) For an in-depth study of all Panin revealed, 'The Last 12 verses of Mark Proof Book' can be read on Openlibrary.org. / Search Ivan Panin. He finishes the book by saying;

"The last twelve verses of Mark are not only a genuine portion of the New Testament, but they are also among its brightest ornaments."

CAN CHRISTIANS BE CURSED?

According to Proverbs 26:2, the answer to that question is no. *Like a fluttering sparrow or a darting swallow, an undeserved curse will not land on its intended victim.* (Living Bible)

The verse implies undeserved curses may be in the air. More than one Church meeting has been visited by the local dark spiritual group, with the intention of applying curses to the Christians. Generally, these groups seem to have the misconception Christians are weak, scared, and powerless. The basic definition of a curse is the sending of an evil spirit to do harm to another person.

Ephesians 1:4 tells us why curses do not land on believers in Jesus. *According as he (God) hath chosen us in him (Jesus) before the foundation of the world, that we should be holy and without blame before him in love. Jesus .... disarmed principalities and powers, and He made a public spectacle of them, triumphing over them by the cross.* (Colossians 2:15) (if you are not a Christian and want the disarming of spiritual powers coming against you, invite Jesus into your life, and you will come under His protection)

In one of his books, Nicky Cruz tells of an incident in one of his Crusade meetings. It was an outdoor event somewhere in the United States. The word of the meetings had reached the dark spiritual groups and they arrived in large numbers, doing all they could to cause evil power to stop the Crusade. I do not remember all the details but in summary; when Nicky Cruz stood to speak large numbers of the dark spiritual groups were afflicted with some sort of breathing problem, and emergency services had to attend. Many were taken to hospital. The Crusade was an enormous success.

That incident is a manifestation of what we are told about ourselves in the New Testament. Paul prayed that we might know...*what is the exceeding greatness of His (God the Father) power toward us who believe, according to the working of His mighty power...* (Ephesians1:19). And *you are of God little children and have overcome them, because greater is He who is in you than he who is in the World.* (1 John 4:4) I had experiences of protection from evil on a much smaller scale during street evangelism.

No matter what our experience of these things is, it is important we are strong in three areas of our lives; refusing to fear, determined faith in God's Word, and proficient in resisting. Here are three verses that cover those topics. *For God has not given us a spirit of fear, but of power and of love and of a sound mind.* (2Timothy 1:7)

Be sober-minded and alert. Your adversary the devil prowls around like a roaring lion, seeking someone to devour. Resist him, standing firm in your faith. (1Peter5:8)

Submit yourselves, then, to God. Resist the devil, and he will flee from you. (James 4:7)

MY EXPERIENCE OF WRONG TEACHING AS A NEW CHRISTIAN

This section is not an exhaustive treatment of correct teaching. Here, I am giving my experience of attempting to make sense of what I was taught as a new Christian. At that time, I should have been studying the Bible for myself. I think I had accepted unconsciously the idea that only Pastor's and Theologians could interpret the Bible correctly. Because of that, I was reading books to find answers to my queries.

I was told I had a sin nature co-existing with God's nature within myself. The problem with that was I could find no reference to Christians having a sin nature anywhere in the New Testament. Romans seven was the so-called proof chapter for that teaching. Paul, in that chapter, does say 'sin that dwells in me' but he adds the explanation 'that is in my flesh.' When I asked the answer was 'oh, that means the sin nature.' Why didn't it say the sin nature then? The context of the whole of chapter seven in a careful reading is Paul talking about his body. He says his inner man desires to do the will of God.

Romans 6: 6 declares we died with Christ 'that the body of sin might be destroyed.' Again, I was told that speaks of the sin nature. If that were true why did it mention the body, and if it had been destroyed how could I still have the sin nature in me? Next was the explanation that the Holy Spirit would convict me of sin. I was to keep short accounts with God. The only reference to the Holy Spirit convicting I could find was in the book of John, where It states the Holy Spirit will convict the World of sin, righteousness, and judgement to come. Christians are not of the World. The New Testament says we have been taken out of the World.

Keeping short accounts with God meant I was to keep an eye upon myself regarding sin and continually be confessing it to God. That implied God's main activity with me was keeping a watch on me for sins. All this was confusing to me. I could never work out when I had sinned. For example, the sin of gluttony. How was I to know when I had eaten too much and crossed over the line to gluttony. I was never sure what needed to be confessed. All these things combined produced a life where I was constantly looking within myself, and my relationship with God was mostly uncertainty whether He was pleased with me or not.

I became more or less obsessed with the word 'victory'. I read many books searching for what I could call victory in my life. I would find a new book and excitedly begin to read, only to be disappointed quickly as I realized it had no answers for me. I have discovered the answers in the New Testament for all these things now, but at the time it took years to sort it all out. I began to get break-through when I read some of John Wesley's books. He did not seem to support the sin nature in Christian's idea. The real breakthrough came in a Bible College lecture on Leviticus.

I knew the various offerings of the Old Testament were types of Jesus' sacrifice for sin. The lecturer was speaking about the trespass offering and the sin offering. The trespass offering was for sins committed, the sin offering was for sin in the priests and the people. I realized Jesus had died not only for sins we have committed, but for sin in us as well. Our sinful self, our sin nature (the Bible has no information about a sin nature – it speaks about the condition of the heart – the heart is the centre of any person) If Jesus paid for it on the cross, then it must cease to exist in me. That was when I knew I had victory regarding sin in all its forms, given to me by Christ. If I had begun by studying the Bible myself, I could have reduced the number of years it took me to understand.

As I said at the beginning, I have attempted here to explain my experience as a new Christian having little knowledge of the Bible.

WHY CHRISTIANS SHOULD DO THE WORKS OF JESUS

To answer that question, we could ask ourselves why Jesus did so many works. (Healing, raising the dead, casting out demons, and miracles} The answer is, although He was the Son of God, most could see only a man. It's interesting to remember Christ had a sinless body. People still missed who He was. If that is how it was with Jesus, how much more will it be for us. Our Christian life is largely invisible to the world. The Kingdom of God is certainly invisible to the world. Can you envisage Jesus limiting Himself to talking, and doing no works? It was His works that revealed who He was. He said often that the works He did proved the Kingdom of God had come among His hearers.

Nicodemus the Pharisee came to Jesus at night, convinced by the healings, miracles, and deliverances he had seen. Jesus passed the baton to us. *"Truly, truly, I say to you, whoever believes in me will also do the works that I do; and greater works than these will he do, because I am going to the Father."* (John 14:12) Truly, truly here can be translated as 'a firm fact,' 'a sure thing.'

Apostle Paul explained the correct preaching of the Gospel. *"...by the power of signs and wonders, by the power of the Spirit of God, so that from Jerusalem and all the way around to Illyricum I have fulfilled the ministry of the Gospel of Christ;* (Romans 15:19) I remember once seeing a well-dressed young man, obviously zealous for the Gospel, standing preaching in the central business district of Melbourne. It was a busy part of the day. I watched for about 10 minutes. Nobody was taking the slightest notice of him. I thought to myself how different it would be if he had said, "Are any of you sick? Come forward and Jesus will heal you."

Of course, that would have taken faith and risk on his part. I have been in that position. God had to remind me "talking won't cut it, demonstration is needed." I know of a Christian man who attended a new Age conference. Representatives of every branch of New Age spirituality made up the audience. This guy had got himself on the list of speakers. When his time came, he walked to the stage and invited sick and crippled people to come up to the front to be healed. He went further and told the audience, that if God did not heal every one of those people, the Gospel of Jesus was not the truth.

The audience watched as every single afflicted person was restored. After that demonstration, every member of the audience prayed to receive Jesus as their Saviour. I know this man did not start out with that sort of boldness. He recognized what God wanted him to do in demonstrating the Gospel. He stepped out by faith and over time his boldness increased to a higher level.

Many Christians have ignored God's instruction and settled for talk and reason, in trying to advance the Gospel. We cannot expect results if we are not doing it God's way. No matter how we feel about it, we must start demonstrating out of pure obedience to the Word of God. The saying 'the journey of a thousand miles starts with one step' applies. You have to be an Adventurer. You have to throw caution to the wind; determined to be among those who love people enough to step out for Jesus. Millions are ignoring the Gospel of Christ because they have never seen a demonstration of its reality and power.

THE LEGITIMATE CHRISTIAN LIFE

Only one Christian life is legitimate; the life Jesus modelled. (John 14:8,9) *Philip said to Him, "Lord, show us the Father, and that will be enough for us." Jesus said to him, "Have I been with you so long, and you still do not know me, Philip? Whoever has seen me has seen the Father. How can you say, 'Show us the Father'?* The life Jesus modelled was a united existence with His Father. He expected Philip to understand that. No doubt He expects the same from us.

If we look back through the book of John, we find Jesus continuously explaining His united life with His Father. Philip had not been listening and it earned him a rebuke. (John 17:21) *...that they all may be one, as You, Father, are in Me, and I in You; that they also may be one in us, that the world may believe that You sent Me.* Here we see Jesus asking His Father to give us the same life He lived on Earth. Every Christian is included; *that they all may be one, as you, Father, are in me, and I in you...*

The word 'one' in this verse means a single number. I heard a missionary tell a story which she claimed was true. India at the time of the assassination of Indira Gandhi, was a place of turmoil. The Hindus were incensed against the Sikh's because it was Indira Gandhi's Sikh bodyguard who had committed the crime. A Sikh scholar found himself alone with a group of Hindu men who intended to kill him. Jesus suddenly appeared surprising them all. He said, "why do you want kill me?" The Hindu's explained they had no malice toward Jesus and only intended to kill the Sikh. Jesus replied, "If you kill him, you kill me. I am him and he is me." The Hindu's ran off. Jesus spent about twenty minutes teaching the Scholar about Himself.

If we live this life, Jesus says, the World will believe the Father sent Him. That is a big statement. The whole World will believe Jesus came from God if we live a life of union with God. Obviously, it demands a commitment from us. A determination to move into the legitimate Christian life.

Apostle Paul attempted to describe his experience of life in union with Jesus. (Galatians 2:20) "*I am crucified with Christ: nevertheless, I live; yet not I, but Christ lives in me: and the life which I now live in this body, I live by the faith of the Son of God, who loved me, and gave himself for me.*" Paul's description here, is in the New Testament so that we may read it and adjust our lives accordingly. It is an unusual verse. Paraphrasing gives clarity.

Paul starts by saying he died at Calvary with Jesus. Yet he still lives, but as a different person, which he describes as 'Christ in me.' He separates this new person from his humanity when he says, 'The life I live in this body.' He then gives the driving force of his new life 'the faith of the Son of God.' Notice it is not faith in the Son of God, but the faith of the Son of God. Paul's union with Jesus is such that he lives by Jesus' faith. He finishes by saying all this is available to him because of Christ's loving atonement.

I purchased a small book that, in its entirety, described a vision the Christian author had been given. One part of the vision, which the author did not comment on, caught my attention. Amid the activity of the vision a mature Christian Elder the author knew, appeared, seated. The image of him was flashing, alternating continually from him to Jesus. As the author looked it was Jesus, then the elder, then Jesus again, then the elder, continuously. I considered that part of the vision as the most important. It was communicating the truth that maturity in the Christian life is unity with Jesus. The same unity Jesus and Paul described.

It surprised me the author did not comment on that part of the vision. He mentioned it and moved on. I wondered how many Christians also miss this central issue of Christian living ?

BEHOLD! I MAKE ALL THINGS NEW

He will wipe away every tear from their eyes, and death shall be no more, neither shall there be mourning, nor crying, nor pain anymore, for the former things have passed away. And the one sitting on the throne said, "behold, I am making everything new!" And then he said to me, "Write this down, for what I tell you is trustworthy and true." (Rev 21:4,5) Two references here identify the one on the throne as Jesus. (1) In chapter twenty the person on the throne is judging. Jesus said the Father has given all judgment to the Son. (John 5:22) (2) The one on the throne refers to Himself, later in Chapter twenty-one, as the Alpha and Omega. Jesus called Himself the Alpha and Omega in Revelation chapter one.

The word 'behold' in today's language means 'look closely at this' or 'give your attention to this.' We are to consider closely the fact Jesus is making all things new (has made all things new - in some translations) It is significant that this statement is made at the end of everything old, and the beginning of everything new. Revelation twenty tells us of the end of death, hades, the devil, the anti-Christ (beast) the false prophet, all whose names are not in the Lambs Book of Life, and the Earth and the sky. Revelation 21:4 gives more detail, declaring the end also of pain, sorrow, crying, and tears. Then sums up all that has ended as 'the former things.

The new Earth and sky appear, as does the Holy City, the new Jerusalem. Revelation 21:3 speaks of a new experience between God and His people on the new Earth, and in the new Jerusalem. We are to consider and understand; all this happens because of Jesus' suffering, death, burial, and resurrection. The earth is cursed because of Adam and Eve's disobedience. (Genesis 3:17) By the same disobedience, we had become unspiritual and slaves to sin. (Romans 7:14)

Jesus' atonement enabled all of creation to be made new. Man was spiritually dead because of sin. God gave Adam dominion over the Earth and everything on it. Through him, the Earth was cursed. Nature and the animal world suffered because of that curse. Jesus' as the second Adam, in His atonement, reversed the entire tragedy. Jesus words "it is finished" on the cross, announced the complete retrieval of all Adam gave away.

We are not yet in full possession of that reversal. Romans eight says we wait for the redemption of our bodies. (Romans 8:23) We will be changed in the twinkling of an eye. (1Cor 15:52) The new Earth and the sky will not appear until all the time periods of the book of Revelation have passed. But it is a sure thing. The suffering, death, burial, and resurrection of Jesus guarantees all things will receive their originality.

"Worthy is the Lamb who was slain; to receive power and riches and wisdom. And strength and honour and glory and blessing." (Revelation 5:12)

HOW DO I KNOW WHAT GOD WANTS ME TO DO?

It was a Christian cruise. Oral Roberts and his wife were on board. One of the male passengers had prayed for a sick young boy and God had healed him. That created a burning question in the mind of the prayer, and he anxiously looked for an opportunity to put the question to Oral Roberts. The opportunity eventually presented itself. "Should I have a healing ministry," he asked? The answer was unexpected, "Ask the little boy."

What was Oral Roberts doing there? He was turning the guy's attention to the need, and away from selfish ambition. It was all ambition in my Christian life for a long time. Did God want me to be a Pastor, Evangelist, or maybe a Prophet? Did I have the gift to preach? Had He chosen me to preach to thousands and see hundreds of souls won to Christ? It took time to get through to me God was not overly interested in my ambition. He wanted me to cooperate with Him to meet the needs of other people.

No doubt Oral Roberts had seen enough desperately sick people in his tent crusades for it to be indelibly impressed upon him; whatever status he held in the body of Christ, it was for one reason, to collaborate with God to help others. Most of us are familiar with the text of Mathew 9:35–38.

Jesus went through all the towns and villages, teaching in their synagogues, proclaiming the good news of the kingdom, and healing every disease and sickness. When He saw the crowds, He had compassion on them, because they were harassed and helpless, like sheep without a shepherd. Then

He said to His disciples, "The harvest is plentiful, but the workers are few. Ask the Lord of the harvest, therefore, to send out workers into His harvest field."

Christ's motivation for the instruction He gave here was His seeing the needs of the people. We could paraphrase 'the harvest is plentiful' as 'people everywhere have needs. God calls the needs of humanity His harvest field. Paul said we are co-laborers with God in the work of the Gospel. God is a laborer in His own harvest field.

Relationship comes first in laboring with God. Romans tells us those led by the Spirit of God are the Sons of God. To be sent to the harvest field of God means to go with God into the work. What does that mean for you and me in hands-on activity? The John 4 version of our verse says, *'lift up your eyes and look on the fields, for they are white unto harvest.'* Some are put into God's harvest by the choice and call of God. The rest of us must take the initiative and begin to look for people in need.

Collaborating with God in His harvest is something to be learned. As with most things, experience increases effectiveness. The New Testament gives us our job description. Heal the sick, raise the dead, cleanse the lepers, cast out demons, preach the Gospel, give and it shall be given to you. With our job description settled we begin to look for people in need. The lady we always see at the mall, who is suffering from severe asthma. The homeless man who does not have enough winter footwear or clothes. The stories that reach us of desperately ill people beyond the help of medicine, the neighbours who are struggling to pay their electricity bill, those in our vicinity with drug addiction problems, and others struggling with mental and emotional issues.

Then we begin to talk to God about these needs that have come to our attention. Who does He want us to approach? How does He want us to go about it? God has a million creative ways to reach suffering humanity. The only qualification required is to be available. It is a good thing to allow ourselves to begin to feel the responsibility we have as Christians to help others.

Other translations of Mathew nine say, '*Ask God to thrust out laborers into His harvest.*' Why not jump into the deep end and pray, 'Lord, thrust me out into your harvest.' That will get things moving!!

HAS BIBLE STUDY BECOME AN EXCUSE ?

A couple of recent conversations got me thinking about the reasons for Bible study. I pointed out the clear Bible answer to a question under discussion in the first conversation. The answer came back; "good point I'll have to study that some more." I thought to myself 'what is there to study? It is written clearly on the page.' The second conversation elicited this response; "I guess I'll learn more about that as God draws me into His truth." I responded, "I don't believe God draws us into His truth. He presents us with it as a whole book, expecting us to read it, believe it, and most importantly, to do it,"

The two answers I received reveal a thought pattern prevalent among Christians, and one that is detrimental to Christian living. Put briefly; you cannot understand the Bible instantly from what is written on the page. Both of the above statements have the underlying implication that you will never get around to doing anything for God until you do more study, or He draws you into His truth over time. The second is a real deception. It puts all the responsibility on God, and excuses me from doing anything at all. It is Ok if I wait my whole life doing nothing, because He has not drawn me sufficiently into His truth.

These ideas have their roots in the Bible College Movement. The American Bible college movement developed in reaction to the secularization of U.S. higher education. The Bible institute/college movement has been described as 'a protest to the inroads of secularization in higher education and as a base for the education of lay workers and full-time Bible teachers, evangelists, and pastors. As one historian put it, "It is not a coincidence that the Bible institute movement grew up during the very period when the philosophy of naturalism became prevalent in American education." Between 1882 and 1920, 39 Bible schools were founded in the United States.

I am not pointing the finger at Bible Colleges, although I do think the supernatural element was not given enough prominence. After all Christian living is all supernatural. Rather, that the idea developed from them, of the need for a secular type of education to succeed in Christian living. It is interesting to note the early founders of Bible Colleges such as Spurgeon, A B Simpson and Moody, were men raised up by God directly. Throughout history all major Christian Ministries have been led by people picked out and supernaturally equipped by God.

The experience of Maria Woodworth Etter underscores my point in this section. She claimed a lack of understanding of the Bible as an excuse not to obey God's leading. A vision of an open Bible appeared on the wall, and thereafter she had a permanent supernatural knowledge of the Bible. Is Study of the Bible endorsed by Scripture? Yes, but it's true meaning needs to be recognized. *Study to shew thyself approved unto God, a workman that needs not to be ashamed, rightly dividing the word of truth.* (2Tim 2:15)

The word study is in the King James Bible. Most other translations use the original language meaning, which paraphrased is; Be eager to make yourself available to God, a laborer who dissects the Word of God correctly. In depth study is not the correct meaning here. Correctly dissecting the Word, in context here, has the idea of a careful surface reading of Scripture, receiving what it says, resulting in a life of action, the only life that gets God's approval.

Nicodemus, a Pharisee, and representative of all the Rabbinical schools of the day who had crowded God out of their lives in favor of intellectual learning, tells us of Jesus' example of the life that pleases God. *There was a man named Nicodemus, a Jewish religious leader who was a Pharisee. He came to Jesus at night and said, "Rabbi, we know that you are a teacher who has come from God. For no one could perform the signs you are doing if God were not with him."* (John 3:1,2)

Christianity is a life of doing, in relationship with God, guided by the revelation given to us in the Bible. The Nike motto applies. Just do it. We should come away from every Bible study with the question in our minds; 'what does God want me to do now'?

CHRISTIAN, YOU CAN WRITE TO A PRISONER

Only one life, it will soon be past. Only what is done for Christ will last.

As Christians, we are called to talk the talk and walk the walk.

Is it God's will for me to write to a prisoner? In Mathew25:36,40 Jesus gives His approval and leaves the choice up to us. Paraphrased it says, *'When you visited those in prison you visited me.'* In many prisons, we can visit through online video meetings, but it starts with writing.

Two websites will get you started in writing to a prisoner in the USA. So far writing prisoners in the USA is the extent of my experience. I live in Australia. The first website is WriteAPrisoner.com.

It is an information website. It has photos of prisoners, men, and women, who want somebody to write to them. It gives their personal prison number, the length of their sentence, and a few lines of comment about themselves. I suggest you ask the Lord who He wants you to write to; then look through the lists.

The second site is https://www.jpay.com. All contact with your prisoner is done through this site. I guess there may be US prisons where you can communicate with inmates by envelope and paper mail. I have done no research in that direction. My guy is in what seems to be a high-security facility. I think you will find all the higher security prisons will only allow contact through jpay.

jpay.com

It is just a matter of entering your email and generating a password to open an account. Entering the prisoner's personal number will bring up information on what facility they are in and whether contact is possible. Contact through jpay is much the same as email. The difference is the need to purchase jpay stamps for each letter sent. Letters cost one stamp; images are one stamp extra each. $5 buys 20 stamps. $10 will get you 60 stamps. Prisoners need stamps to reply. A box is ticked to transfer one stamp to the inmate for reply.

Here are a few points I have learned after six months of jpay letters to my friend.

Do not expect too much. Reading and writing may not be your recipient's forte. Allow time for the contact to develop. Letters should be around ten lines and kept to a light and friendly tone. All letters in and out are scrutinized.

Start with a 1Corinthians 13 attitude. 'Love is patient, love is kind, love does not notice a wrong done etc. Know you are doing something that pleases God. A short letter regularly sent can mean a lot to a prisoner. Be consistent and always keep your word. If you say I will write again on Wednesday, be certain to do it. Over time the inmate will accept you as a genuine person they can trust.

My friend earns a small amount of money working in the prison laundry. Previous to my contact he could only afford a few stamps to contact his family occasionally. Jpay allows me to transfer stamps to him which in turn means he can purchase other things with his earnings and have increased contact with family and friends.

His facility allows books to be sent from one online retailer and a second-hand bookshop 'Edward Hamilton Books.' Prisons have libraries but access to books is slow and borrowing time seems to be short. I have sent books he requested and have included the occasional Christian book among them.

Inevitably questions will come to your mind. 'Is this guy telling me the truth?' 'Is he just saying what he thinks I want to hear?' 'Is he just using me to get more stamps etc?' The answer to that is to not take it too seriously, maintain a 1Corinthians 13 attitude, talk to God about the contact, and use your inner wisdom. Jesus knew prisoners are not perfect people. They are in prison for a reason. If we write, we are showing our concern for another human being in need. Prison is not a fun place for anybody. We may have to take any good we do by faith.

Jesus equated contacting (visiting) a prisoner with visiting Him. That puts it, for me, high on the list of things to do.

REASONS A CHRISTIAN SHOULD WRITE TO A PRISONER

The overarching reason Christians should write to a prisoner, is because the prison population worldwide is a harvest field. I am referring to the harvest fields Jesus spoke about in John 4:35,36; *"You know the saying, 'Four months between planting and harvest.' But I say, wake up and look around. The fields are already ripe for harvest. The harvesters are paid good wages, and the fruit they harvest is people brought to eternal life. What joy awaits both the planter and the harvester alike."* And Mathew 9:27,28; He said to his disciples, *"The harvest is great, but the workers are few. So, pray to the Lord who is in charge of the harvest; ask him to send more workers into his fields."*

Prisons are full of people who would never have paid any attention to the message of the Gospel of Christ if they had not been sent to prison. It sounds strange to say but a prison sentence was the best thing that could have happened to many of them. It has spared many from a life cut short by wrong life choices. The tedium of a prison sentence forces a person to think about the life they have chosen to live, who they are, and why they do what they do. The list is exceedingly long of true stories of men and women who accepted Jesus in prison and had their lives transformed.

Time in prison often brings regret, and the resolve to change. A prison sentence brings life and independence to a grinding halt. God looks upon the prison population and sees a harvest field. It also presents God with a problem. Jesus described it when He said, *"the harvest is plentiful, but the laborers are few. Pray therefore the Lord of the harvest, that He* might thrust out laborers into His harvest." For want of a better way of saying it, God has a lot of prisoners right where He wants them. Forced to evaluate their lives and having the motivation and ample quiet time to hear His voice.

In my early days as a Christian in New Zealand, I heard a Maori Evangelist tell how he had visited a prison, talked with, and prayed for the prisoners. After he left some of the prisoners heard God speaking directly to them while alone in their cells. One man told him he heard a voice saying, "when are you going to give your life to me?" The important thing to note is, that it happened after the Evangelist had visited, preached, and prayed. The New Testament pattern for people finding Jesus as Savior is; a Christian goes, speaks, and prays. God does the rest.

Our resonsibility is to make ourselves available to contact prisoners at God's leading. Our job is to have faith that God can do wonderful things in the lives of prisoners, through our simple contact. I remember, in my low self-esteem- as a new Christian, how relieved I felt when I realized God was only asking me to be a laborer. Laborers are not highly skilled workers. They are everyday people with little training, who make themselves available to an employer for basic work.

We should follow Jesus's instruction to ask God to send laborers into this harvest field. Of course, if you start praying that way it is highly likely God will say; "why don't you write to a prisoner."

DEMENTIA DEFEATED

I bought the book 'Keeping the Fire' by Rolland Baker a few years ago. I thought I might learn something. I knew Rolland and his wife Heidi were the founders of Iris Ministries in the African country of Mozambique. Mozambique, at that time, was officially the most impoverished country in the World. By all reports, it was a brutal place, saturated with spiritual evil.

God had called Heidi and Rolland to take the Gospel of Jesus' miraculous power of spiritual good to the people of Mozambique. There would be spiritual battles. I figured a man willing to go to the front lines for God, would have something to teach me. Rolland's Mother and Father were Missionaries to Tibet from 1911–1919, to China from 1919 -1950, and Taiwan 1955–1971. They began a Rescue Mission for street children in Yunnan Province, China. The children in the home, mostly boys aged from six to eighteen, began to have spiritual experiences, seeing Heaven through a series of visions. These visions were recounted in the Baker's book 'Visions Beyond the Veil,' which is still available.

I do not recall much about Rollands book because I stopped reading it about halfway through. At that halfway mark I came across something astonishing. The author began to tell how he had been afflicted with dementia and reduced to a state where he did not know where he was and could do nothing for himself. He slipped the testimony in while talking about other things. I remember thinking 'I have been reading this well-written book by this man, after the onset of dementia'!!

The following is part of a transcript of a video where Rolland tells of the experience in his own words,

"Three months ago, I couldn't tie my shoes, I couldn't put my pants on, I put my shirts on backwards or inside out. I could not take a shower, could not dress myself, could not do anything but sleep 22 hours a day. My memory was completely gone. I could not remember three words in a row I did not know what Country I was in. The doctor said I had very advanced serious vascular dementia and that because of that I would be dying soon. Heidi called up my son and my daughter Krystal and Elijah, telling them to quickly fly out to Africa and say goodbye to their dad because they would never know him again. That's where I was three months ago."

"Three months ago, a pastor Wayne (full name missing) from Germany heard about me through our mutual friend Mel Tari, and he refused to accept what the doctors had said. It was just sheer raw faith, and they took me to Germany. They have a kind of a Christian community there. It is a group of Christians that live together and do everything together all through the week. They pray together, they worship together, they have a first-class facility there and they just took me in free and they just started loving on me."

"Every day just pure love. Just the opposite of what the doctors were saying. The doctors had no faith. I was dealing with Christian doctors, and I didn't find one that had any faith that I would be okay, but these Christians took me in." {They gave him health food, exercise, health spa, fruit and vegetable juices, massage, sports, having fun, watching movies, and praying together)

"Exactly what did the trick? It was faith because as soon as I got to Germany, I started remembering things, it was just the sheer love of God, and every week I kept getting better and better and with less medication. I got off the medication." **unquote**

He goes on to say he is back to normal {he authored the book} They use a small plane to get around in Mozambique because of the need to travel long distances over difficult terrain and through the jungle. Shortly before speaking on the video, he had gone for his bi-annual pilot's license test and was complimented by the instructor on his flying skill.

Iris Ministries have books still available, talking about their work over the years they have been in Mozambique. Something I did get from this book is the five principles Rolland says Iris Ministries operate under.

Find God.

Depend on miracles.

Go to the least.

Suffer for Him if necessary.

Rejoice in the Lord.

The video mentioned above is on YouTube. Search 'Rolland Baker Healed.'

FROM WITCH-DOCTORS SON TO CHRISTIAN PROPHET

I thought of naming this article 'The surprising life of Surprise Sithole'. His parents were surprised to see a patch of white hair on his head at birth and named him Surprise. His Mother and Father were witch doctors in a small village in a remote and impoverished area of Mozambique, South-eastern Africa. Surprise was the seventh child of the family. He had never heard of Jesus. Life was hard. Hunger and starvation were a constant threat. In his fifteenth year, he was awakened at night from sleep on the floor of the family hut, by a voice calling his name. As he lay there thinking about the experience, the voice spoke his name again -louder this time and with more intensity.

This time Surprise answered, "who are you, what do you want? The strong masculine voice responded, "get out of the house. If you do not leave you will die." And again, "Surprise you must leave, now!" The voice was loud and seemed to him to make the ground tremble. Looking around he saw his parents and sister were still sleeping. He was the only one hearing the voice. He jumped to his feet, dressed quickly, and walked out into the African night. He made for the house of his best friend Gafar, a boy slightly older than Surprise. After waking his friend, he told him of the events in his home, and that he planned to leave the village. The older boy agreed to accompany him. Together they hurried off into the jungle.

The boys walked for two weeks, finally reaching a village where Mr. Lucas, a Christian man, was waiting for them. God had told him to look out for the two travellers. Eventually, Mr. Lucas led the boys in a prayer to receive Jesus as Savior. It was around this time Surprise heard his entire family had been poisoned by a rival witch doctor group. None survived. Gafar and Surprise became avid soul winners, leaving Mr. Lucas and traveling wherever seemed right to them, preaching the Gospel.

God called them to the Country of Malawi. Many times, they established Churches and moved on. Sometimes God gave Surprise the supernatural ability to preach the Gospel in languages he had never learned. When that miracle happened, Surprise was able to continue to speak that language, He learned English that way. Eight people have been raised from the dead through Surprise's Ministry. It became obvious Surprise had been given a Prophetic Ministry. He came in contact with Roland and Heidi Baker of Iris Ministries in Mozambique and joined their work.

At present I believe Surprise Sithole is touring the world preaching, teaching, and holding revivals. His small book available online is '*A Voice in the Night*'. He is the subject of five or six videos online.

THE SECRET, A BIBLICAL PARADOX

We are all captivated by a secret. It is the reason mystery stories are popular. The advertising industry plays upon our attraction to mystery, in many and varied ways. Sherlock Holmes remains the foremost of fictional detectives due to his reputation as a solver of mysteries. An unraveller of secrets.

If you wanted to explain the theme of the entire Bible to somebody in a few words, you would be right on the mark if you said, "it is about a secret." Colossians 1:27 in the New Testament says *to whom God did will to make known what is the riches of the glory of this secret among the nations - which is Christ in you, the hope of the glory.*

Strong's Bible Greek 3466: μυστηρίου (mystēriou) From a derivative of muo; a secret or mystery.

Strong's Bible Hebrew:4565. מִסְתָּר (mistar) Phonetic Spelling: (mis-tawr) secret place, hiding place

The above verse says it is a mystery or secret God wants known among the nations. God desires all people everywhere to know this secret. I was at the mall today having a coffee and watching people go about their daily business. Ordinary people like me, doing the ordinary things we all need to do to live. We, at this mall, were a microcosm of the nations that populate the earth. I wondered how many of those I was watching had the secret. From a distance, superficially, it is not obvious who has the secret.

Jesus said at the culmination of all things God will divide the nations into two groups. Some will be directed to His left and some to His right.

On the right will be those who have the secret, on the left those who do not. The above verse explains the secret. *To whom God did will to make known what the riches of the glory of this secret among the nations - which is Christ in you, the hope of the glory.*

Adam Clark explains the details of the secret in his Commentary of Colossians 1:27: "We find here the sum and substance of the apostle's preaching. He preached Christ, as the only Savior of sinners. He proclaimed this Christ as being in them; for the design of the Gospel is to put men in possession of the Spirit and power of Christ, to make them partakers of the Divine nature, and thus prepare them for an eternal union with Himself. Should it be said that the preposition εν should be translated among, it amounts to the same; for Christ was among them, to enlighten, quicken, purify, and refine them, and this he could not do without dwelling in them.

He preached this present and indwelling Christ as the hope of glory; for no man could rationally hope for glory who had not the pardon of his sins, and whose nature was not sanctified; and none could have pardon but through the blood of His cross; and none could have glorification but through the indwelling, sanctifying Spirit of Christ." **unquote**

The fascinating thing about this verse, and all the information in the Bible on the secret; it is a classic example of paradox. (Something having seemingly contradictory qualities) We are reading an open secret. Whether it be a Gideon Bible in a Hotel room, a battered Bible in a second-hand bookshop, a new Bible in a Christian bookshop, the family Bible handed down through generations, or the many Bibles in local libraries, they all contain the open secret. The word 'know' in the New Testament means 'to experience.' God wishes each of us to know the secret. Christ in you, your only hope of glory.

DAVID HUME DISREGARDS THE GOSPEL OF JESUS CHRIST

David Hume: 1711 — 1776 was a Scottish Enlightenment philosopher, historian, economist, librarian, and essayist, who is best known today for his highly influential system of philosophical empiricism, scepticism, and naturalism.

A well-known quote by Hume. "It is no miracle that a man, seemingly in good health, should die on a sudden: because such a kind of death, though more unusual than any other, has yet been frequently observed to happen. But it is a miracle, that a dead man should come to life, because that has never been observed in any age or country. There must, therefore, be a uniform experience against every miraculous event, otherwise, the event would not merit that appellation. And as a uniform experience amounts to a proof, there is here a direct and full proof, from the nature of the fact, against the existence of any miracle; nor can such a proof be destroyed, or the miracle rendered credible, but by an opposite proof, which is superior." **unquote**

Hume's quote is an 'a priori' conclusion. A conclusion rooted in theory, not in evidence. It could be paraphrased as, 'this is true because I want it to be true.' Hume expected his readers to accept what he had written as truth. He ignored the equivalent written record in the Bible of multiple resurrections from the dead.

The Bible declares the abolition of death and revealing of immortality, as the reason for Jesus Christ's incarnation. *This has now been made evident through the appearing of our Savior Christ Jesus, who has abolished death and has brought life and immortality to light through the gospel.* (2Timothy 1;9) The written record of the Gospels intention is the true enlightenment. Naming a rejection of the Bible's written record as the enlightenment is a complete misnomer. Jesus established that basic of the Gospel, by His resurrection from the dead.

Along with the Bibles record, any genuine researcher will find manifold written, video, and podcast, records of Christian resurrections from death, in history and up to the present day. Sceptic Frank Morison set out to prove the resurrection of Christ was a myth and had to accept the New Testament record as true. He tells of his research in a book 'Who Moved the Stone,' available from online retailers and Bookshops.

Harvard Geneticist Richard Lewontin speaking of Scientism, was unexpectedly honest when he said, "We take the side of science because we have an a priori commitment to materialism. Our willingness to accept scientific claims that are against common sense is the key to an understanding of the real struggle between science and the supernatural. Materialism is absolute, we cannot allow a divine foot in the door."

SETTING THE RECORD STRAIGHT

This article is a response to comments I read recently challenging the veracity of the Bible.

Comment: I am better to trust Stephen Hawking's statement that science offers a far better explanation for everything than the idea of God and the ancient myths of the Bible.

Psalm 22:29 *All the rich of the earth will feast and worship; all who go down to the dust will kneel before him — those who cannot keep themselves alive.*

Comment: The Bible is total superstition and creation myth. (Superstition means excessively credulous belief in and reverence for the supernatural)

Most of the Bible is an undeniable record of the history of the Jewish people. Psalm 2:12 *Serve the LORD with fear and rejoice with trembling. Kiss the Son, lest He be angry, and your way will lead to your destruction, when His wrath ignites in an instant. Blessed are all who take refuge in Him.*

Comment: It is poor logic to rely on the Bible instead of Scientific discovery.

Proverbs 14:12 *There is a way which seems right to a man, but the end thereof are the ways of death.*

Comment: The Bible never revealed any cure for any disease.

Exodus 15:26 *"If you listen carefully to the LORD your God and do what is right in his eyes, if you pay attention to his commands and keep all his decrees, I will not bring on you any of the diseases I brought on the Egyptians, for I am the LORD, who heals you."*

Comment: The Bible never revealed any scientific fact that was unknown prior to its writing.

Moses wrote the previously unknown scientific facts about creation, 300 years after the event.

Comment: While some like to hold up some vaguely worded things written in scripture as prophecy of future events, Nostradamus has far exceeded the bible's "hit rate" for forecasting future events.

From 'Reasons to Believe' website. Approximately 2,500 prophecies appear in the pages of the Bible, about 2,000 of which already have been fulfilled to the letter — no errors. Regarding Nostradamus, the opposite of the comment is true. Everybody has heard of Nostradamus, but few can tell of any accurate predictions. Although his book has never been out of print, the so-called predictions are so vague that the reader must work hard to see anything in them.

Comment: The Earth is not older than the Sun

Genesis, one reveals the Earth to be much older than our present Sun. The Earth was in existence before Genesis one. Our present Sun was created on the fourth creation day.

Comment: Human sperm is not seed.

The word seed is translated 'offspring' in many translations. The original Hebrew includes 'sperm,' 'children' 'posterity' in its meaning.

Comment: Biblical authors knew nothing of discovered scientific facts.

That is obviously true. In their relationship with the one who created all things, they were able to demonstrate dominion over the material realm far surpassing mere scientific knowledge. EG; Moses causing water to come from a rock, the parting of the red sea, healing of leprosy, the dead raised, the Egyptian plagues, water consumed by supernatural fire, and many more.

Comment: There is absolutely no reason to think that the Bible is of divine origin, and, in fact, there is no reason to believe in the divine altogether. It is all superstition.

I have answered the first part of the comment. Regarding the second part, Romans 1:20 *For since the creation of the world God's invisible qualities — his eternal power and divine nature — have been clearly seen, being understood from what has been made, so that people are without excuse.*

Psalm 14:1 .... *the fool says in his heart 'there is no God.'* I add here that most of us were this type of fool at some time in our lives.

A READY MADE, HOLY HIGHWAY

American Standard Version. (Isaiah 35: 8 –10) *And a highway shall be there, and a way, and it shall be called The way of holiness; the unclean shall not pass over it; but it shall be for the redeemed: the wayfaring men, yea fools, (another translation says, 'whoever walks the road though a fool, shall not go astray')(some translations add 'simple minded' here) shall not err therein.*

No lion shall be there, nor shall any ravenous beast go up thereon; they shall not be found there; but the redeemed shall walk there. And the ransomed of Jehovah shall return and come with singing unto Zion; and everlasting joy shall be upon their heads: they shall obtain gladness and joy, and sorrow and sighing shall flee away.

Isaiah (Hebrew: יְשַׁעְיָהוּ, Yəšaʿyāhū, "Yahweh is Salvation") was the 8th-century BC Israelite Prophet after whom the Book of Isaiah is named. Written around 740 BC, this section of Isaiah is a prophecy of the New Testament Christian life. The verses have valuable information to challenge erroneous ideas about living for Jesus, which have hindered many Christians from living a full victorious life in Christ.

The simple heading for those teachings is 'self-effort teachings;' I must work to make my heart pure; I must work to make myself more like Christ. The problem there is, Jesus said our flesh profits nothing. What does this have to do with the Holy Highway?

Two facts stand out to me in these verses. The Holy Highway is for the redeemed to walk upon. The metaphor of a Highway already constructed, is used; *a Highway shall be there.* The finished Highway waits for the redeemed to use it. It speaks of a holy Christian life provided for us by Jesus. The foundation of a holy life is the pure heart given to us by Christ's atonement. Acts fifteen teaches us, when the Holy Spirit came upon Cornelius's people, they received a pure heart.

A final blow lands on the self - effort teaching in the statement, *even fools and the simple minded can succeed at holy living.* Human intelligence, skill, or energy, is no aid to holy living. Anyone with the ability to accept Jesus as Saviour, and a pure heart, will be enabled by God to live a holy life. They are kept by the power of God through faith.

The pure heart within us is the Holy Highway, unreachable by lions and ravenous beasts. This is the life where all things are made new.

THE PURPOSE OF LIFE IS TO BE SAVED

This week I looked at a book by Author and Medium member Lara Tigler MD entitled 'You're Saved.' (Available online) It is a great book, by the way, to give to somebody who doesn't see a reason to consider Christianity. She begins the book by saying the purpose of life is to be saved. In my years as a Christian that had never occurred to me. The purpose of life is to be saved. Why? Because eternity is a long time. Ecclesiastes 3:11 says *'God has set eternity in the heart of man.'*

Arthur Malcolm Stace (9 February 1885/30 July 1967) known as Mr. Eternity, was an Australian soldier. He was an alcoholic from his teenage years until the early 1930s, when he converted to Christianity and began to spread his message by inscribing the word "Eternity" in copperplate writing with yellow chalk on footpaths and doorsteps in and around Sydney, from Martin Place to Parramatta, from 1932 to his death in 1967.

The human soul is eternal. The body dies and disintegrates, but the soul remains for eternity. If we die without God, the soul enters eternity without God. If we die in a relationship with God the Father, Jesus, and the Holy Spirit, the soul enjoys eternity with God. Someone described eternity this way; imagine a steel ball the size of the Earth. A fly lands on the ball once every million years. When the steel ball has worn away by the friction of the fly's landings, eternity has just begun. Eternity is a long time.

Eternity is the continuous, never-ending state, of now. Time does not exist in eternity. It is always the immediate present. No past, no future. We could rephrase 'the purpose of life is to be saved' this way; God is allowing life on Earth to continue because He wants as many saved as possible. Obviously, the most critical issue for any person is their need to enter eternity with God, whether they recognize it or not.

Acts 1: 7 records Jesus speaking to the twelve disciples. *And He said to them, "It is not for you to know the times or seasons which the Father has put in His own authority"* Have you ever considered the problem God has? When to bring everything to a close. If it happened today, millions would miss eternity in heaven with God. We can lighten God's burden by being available to His instruction, in reaching those who have not received the Gospel of Jesus. Many answers would be forthcoming if we asked people the purpose of their lives; to be wealthy, to be happy, to set their children up for life, sport, academic achievement, to have a good time, to win the Nobel prize, to be known as the best in my chosen profession, to make life better for future generations, and many more.

The New Testament tells us the devil has blinded the minds of those who do not believe the Gospel of Jesus, with the intention of keeping them from spending eternity with God. Eternity is the main issue for everybody. All I have said here is encapsulated in one verse in the New Testament. *For God so loved the World that He even gave up His only Son, so that whoever believes in Him, should not perish (eternity without God) but have everlasting life. (John 3:16)*

I have decided, whenever I get the chance, by God's grace, to tell people the purpose of life is to be saved.